country   India   Hindu   religion individual castes /S.C/S.T / O.B.C weaker   sections   immediate   - poverty solution, increase huge business , industry ,tender ,social empowerment ,human right very- very big role join individual castes sufficient   number   lawyer (LL.B/LL.M) and medicine graduate /postgraduate   degree(MBBS/MD)/profession

EDITION-3,JANUARY 2015

country India Hindu religion individual castes /S.C/S.T / O.B.C weaker sections immediate - poverty solution, increase huge business , industry ,tender ,social empowerment ,human right very-very big role join individual castes sufficient number lawyer (LL.B/LL.M) and medicine graduate /postgraduate degree(MBBS/MD)/profession

ISBN: - 978-1-312-82815-5,

Edition-3(low price edition,
 PremiumPaperback, Perf-ect
Bound Paperback

,JANUARY-2015

Publisher company- http://www.lulu.com- Lulu Press, Inc. 3101 Hillsborough Street, Raleigh, NC 27607,CAROLINA ,UNITED STATE OF AMERICA

ISBN:-978-1-312-82815-5

AUTHOR-BIOGRAPHY
AUTHOR NAME - MANTU KUMAR SATYAM
COUNTRY- INDIA ,STATE –JHARKHAND

RELIGION-HINDU,CATEGORY-0.B.C(WEAKER SECTION),CASTE-SUNDI(O.B.C WEAKER SECTION) ,DATE OF BIRTH-21/04/1984 COMPLETE ADD- S/O-.SHIV PRSAD MANDAL, FRONT BAIDYNATH TRADING/ HARDWARE,CHOICE EMPORIUM SHOP BUILDING ,NEAR JAMUNA JOUR POOL, NEAR RAMJANKI MANDIR , SARWAN/ SARATH MAIN ROAD,,DEOGHAR,DISTRICT-DEOGHAR,STATE-

JHARKHAND,COUNTRY-
INDIA,PINCODE-814112 .   .

MY OTHER PERMANENT ADD-

VILL–SUKHJORA,POST-
BAMANDIHA,BLOCK-
.
SARATH,DIST-DEOGHAR,STATE-
JHARKHAND ,COUNTRY-INDIA

EDUCATION- 1. B.SC(PHY HONS)
FROM   DEOGHAR   COLLEGE
,DEOGHAR   S.K.M.U UNIVERSITY,
DUMKA   ,STATE-
JHARKHAND,COUNTRY-INDIA
2.M.SC CRRA COMPLETE   SMU-
DE   UNIVERSITY   , SYNDICATE
HOUSE ,MANIPAL ,STATE –
KARNATAK,COUNTRY-INDIA.
(SESSION-2010-12) ,ROLL
NUMBER-671016791.

3.   2   YEARS
POST   GRADUATE   DIPLOMA
HUMAN RIGHTS COMPLETE FROM
INDIAN   INSTITUTE   OF   HUMAN
RIGHTS ,
A-50,PARYAVARAN

COMPLEX ,SAKET MADAINGARHI MARG,NEW DELHI, 110030,INDIA COUNTRY-INDIA(SESSION 2012-14), ROLL NUMBER-384/HR/2012

DEDICATION-
BOOKS DEDICATE TO LNDIAN
INSTITUTE OF HUMAN RIGHTS
,A-50,PARYAVARAN COMPLEX
,SAKET MADAINGARHI MARG,
,NEW DELHI, 110030,INDIA
SESSION-2012-14).

ITS CONTENT
HAVE THE PARTS OF MY
MASTER THESSIS AWARD –
ROLE OF NATIONAL HUMAN
RIGHT COMMISSION NEW
DELHI,INDIA PROTECTION OF
HUMAN RIGHTS IN INDIA HAVE
COMPLETE FROM INDIAN
INSTITUTE OF HUMAN RIGHTS
,A-50,PARYAVARAN COMPLEX
,SAKET MADAINGARHI MARG,
,NEW DELHI, 110030,INDIA
SESSION-2012-14) UNDER THE
COMPLETE OF MY 2 YEARS
POST GRADUATE DIPLOMA
HUMAN RIGHTS COMPLETE FROM
INDIAN INSTITUTE OF HUMAN
RIGHTS ,A-50,PARYAVARAN
COMPLEX ,SAKET MADAINGARHI
MARG,
NEW DELHI, 110030, INDIA ,
COUNTRY-INDIA(SESSION 2012-
14)

subjects introduction

1. country india hindu religion individual castes /s.c/s.t / o.b.c weaker sections immediate - poverty solution, increase huge business , industry ,tender ,social empowerment ,human right very-very big role join individual castes sufficient number **lawyer (LL.B/LL.M) and medicine graduate /postgraduate degree(like MBBS/MD)/profession**

2. in country india hindu religion individual castes /.s.c /s.t o.b.c weaker sections so- cialjustice /empowerment, economic development increase role of politicians with comparison with judiciary system with support lawyer medicine graduate /postgraduate degree(like MBBS/MD)/profession

3.
bureaucracy in country india in reference of
hindu religion individual castes increase social empowerment

,business, economic development comparison on sufficient number lawyer

(LL.B/LL.M) and medicine graduate /postgraduate degree(like MBBS/MD)/profession

4.gangster composition in india /which hindu religion individual castes have join sufficient number lawyer (LL.B/LL.M) and medicine graduate /postgraduate degree(like MBBS/MD)/profession and safety of concerned problem

1.country india, hindu religion individual castes,o.b.c weaker sections,s.c/s.t immediate poverty solution,increase economic development ,
industry,tender,social empowerment very-very big role join individual castes sufficient number lawyer(ll.b/ll.m) and medicine (mbbs/md) degree/profession
Country india hindu religion individual castes sufficient number lawyer (LL.B/LL.M) and medicine graduate /postgraduate degree(like MBBS/MD)/profession face all political problem arise in
 development , have not any problem of social security. .its have to
Theoretical understand by indian constitution and

Practical understand to see in picture of india .

In country india hindu religion any caste /individual castes sufficient number of lawyer (LL.B/LL.M) and medicine graduate /postgraduate degree(like MBBS/MD)/profession or profession very big and very-Very important role of advancement or development, power and business are in social structure. In

reference of other profession officers and politicians very - very small role or huge difference comparison than lawyer (LL.B/LL.M) and medicine graduate /postgraduate degree(like MBBS/MD)/profession hindu religion complicated caste structure of caste development , power and business.

if individual castes have sufficient number of 10% lawyer (LL.B/LL.M) and medicine graduate /postgraduate degree(like MBBS/MD)/profession the casts benefit of 10% of sufficient number.

Its important in other word say it, in country india, hindu religion general caste or any other caste to now time do huge scale of business , govt. Tender, land owner e.t.c .have not possible of without sufficient number of lawyer and m.b.b.s /m.d/(medicine graduate /post graduate) degree Of individual general castes, hindu religion,india for the maintain of caste power, advancement /development, social empowerment like huge scale of business ,land owner and govt. Tender

.without sufficient number. Of lawyer (LL.B/LL.M) and medicine graduate /postgraduate degree(like MBBS/MD)/profession hindu religion ,general caste/and other huge scale of business, country india(due to same of complicated hindu religion ,caste social structure in india) have many Factors /issue arises of huge scale business ,huge scale land owner ,govt. Tender e.t.c. Its have to said very-very big problem or have not possible.

also it have to say in deep of collaboration of one caste to other caste, hindu religion ,country india have sufficient number of lawyer and m.b.b.s /m.d/m.s. In some cases it have to seen . Increase of business but it have not increase of own caste power without sufficient number Of lawyer l.l.b/l.l.m and medicine (like MBBS/MD) graduate /postgraduate degree
In under of the self/own hindu religion (less population castes),country india of complicated caste structure face very - very basic problem of life concerned of other then development without sufficient
number lawyer (LL.B/LL.M) and medicine graduate /postgraduate degree(like MBBS/MD)/profession

its have not any advantage of more people and its benefit of other profession like politicians and officers very- very small chances to join of politicians and officers (few number) two or three) rather then more peoples caste thousands to thousands.

it also have to be seen census of india of hindu religion caste development in social structure with time.
it have to be seen in country india hindu religion scenario less population caste have to huge benefit in some year join the sufficient number of lawyer l.l.b/l.l.m and medicine (MBBS/MD) graduate /postgraduate degree
 more development like power business complicated caste social structure rather then s.c/ s.t join the profession politicians and officers in long to long time /year in same conditions. also they caste have good manage of land owner in caste participate already in past time land

have not exist but acquire rather then s.c and s.t. it have to understand on the concept of constitution of country india in political power increase (in political power hidden of economic power) of backward caste in hindu religion reservation of politicians and officers.

in the point of the view north india yadav caste have some good number of ll.b/ll.m (lawyer) but not sufficient number.

.also kurmi caste in bihar/jharkhand combine have some number of lawyers. also have some few number of MBBS .(medicine graduate degree)

its have theoretical under stand by country india constitution and also seen in practical .the judiciary is third

pillar of indian democracy and control the implementation work

2 to 3 level implementation work 1.basics level 2.standard level to higher level .

the standard level to higher level social justice social empowerme--nt promote of

standard level business to higher level, and to promote of work or complexity produce of which castes hindu castes sufficient number of lawyer (LL.B/LL.M) and medicine (MBBS/MD) graduate /postgraduate degree/profession have not solve by the issue by politicians and officers
.its issue have to solve by which castes have sufficient
number lawyer (LL.B/LL.M) and medicine (MBBS/MD) graduate /postgraduate degree/profession .there for role of lawyer (LL.B/LL.M) and medicine (MBBS/MD) graduate /postgraduate degree/profession in constitution.

also country india hindu religion individual castes on development point middle level to higher level bussiness , industry ,tender land owner manage not possible without hindu religion individual castes join sufficient number lawyer (LL.B/LL.M) and medicine (MBBS/MD) graduate /postgraduate degree/profession .

its have to understand concerned mention on detail of the matter.
s.c /s.t take 50 to 60 years take to basic   level social justice/social empowerment .but

not a problem of skills of people but skills of problem of degree.
but which country india hindu religion weaker section individual castes join sufficient number lawyer (LL.B/LL.M) and medicine (MBBS/MD   )   graduate /postgraduate degree   solve standard   level   to   higher level social   justice/empowerment to promote of work in business /industry very easily in 4 to 5 years.

note-in the point of view in country india   lawyer (LL.B/LL.M)   and medicine   graduate /postgraduate degree(like   MBBS/MD)/profession not meaning of only court and medicine practice (only) but also have self business by person occupied the degree more to more

effective /efficient due to key point /key master of caste

power, bussiness, govt. tender.)

2. in country india hindu religion individual castes /.s.c /s.t o.b.c weaker sections economic development/social empowerment increase role of politicians with comparison with judiciary system support with medicine graduate /postgraduate degree(like MBBS/MD)/profession

in country india hindu religion individual castes .s.c/s.t o.b.c weaker
sections socialjustice /empowerment role of politicians
its issue have to understand by country india constitution theoreticaly and have to seen practicaly. hindu religion individual castes to common people in social justice/ empowerment,economic development 2 to 3 types first basic social justice or basic humanity and 2nd t0 3rd standrd level socialjustice/empowerment to higher level to promote big scale business ,industory, economic development big scale tender and land owner e.t.c
In social justice /empowerment
Politicians make policy in favour

of which castes belong. Issue arise in parliament to asembelly . Also help to media for the point

debate for other politicians ,officers ,and social activist and public awarness. If its have not possible going on people on assemble protest with castes political activist , people to Solve issue under constitution. In the matter its have successful .
They also observe in implementation .of government work what right or wrong with policy of the castes development. Take people on assemble protest but its have solve only basic level social justice /empowerment, economic development in implementation of work issue .but have not to solve by politicians further then basic level level social justice /empowerment, economic development of cases common people due to more complex problem create by which castes/castes lobbing have sufficient number lawyer (LL.B/LL.M) and medicine graduate

/postgraduate degree(like MBBS/MD)/profession
its have to understand by country india constitution or power of judiciary. in practically s.c /s.t take 60 years to reach in basic social justice/ empowerment,economic development . but which weaker section castes join sufficient number lawyer (LL.B/LL.M) and

.

medicine graduate /postgraduate degree(like MBBS/MD)/profession solve standard level to higher level social justice/ empowerment to promote of work in business /industry very easily in 4 to 5 years .

therefore have to say only politicians and officers have not possible to manage business , economic development industry in good way or standard Level social justice to higher level social justice.

3.Bureaucracy in country INDIA in reference of HINDU religion individual castes increase social empowerment economic development comparison on lawyer (LL.B/LL.M) and medicine graduate /postgraduate degree(like MBBS/MD)/profession

its have to understand by country india constitution theoretical and in the country have to see practical understand .

in country india hindu religion which caste have sufficient no. of lawyer and m.b.b.s/m.d/m.s ,which castes bureaucracy/officer have to give the pressure on govt. or say it stop the progress of file due to which castes face more problem have not basics facility of large no. of people like land owner ,business ,employment position, for the concerned of major file progress stop say it like politicians.

.

for major file also flash in news and many time oppose the officers for above mention bureaucracy which hindu castes in country india politicians have sufficient number lawyer (LL.B/LL.M) and medicine graduate /postgraduate degree(like MBBS/MD)/profession indirectly support of the problem.

but problem it fight against bureaucracy reality in ground level which people have face the problem. which hindu castes in country have not sufficient number lawyer (LL.B/LL.M) and medicine graduate /postgraduate degree(like MBBS/MD)/profession fight on ground level against bureaucracy .also same above mention say it for individual people file not major community group development concerned file.

officers which hindu castes in country india have sufficient no. of lawyer have more resistance to fight against cases . Also give the more many type

pressure backward castes people have not sufficient number lawyer (LL.B/LL.M) and medicine graduate /postgraduate degree(like MBBS/MD)/profession to have not done cases against the officers in which hindu castes have not sufficient number lawyer (LL.B/LL.M) and medicine graduate /postgraduate degree(like MBBS/MD)/profession due to environment pressure of stop the progress of file which by the pressure of which hindu castes sufficient number lawyer (LL.B/LL.M) and medicine graduate /postgraduate degree(like MBBS/MD)/profession country india constitution bureuacracy have done implementation of work also secretory level to suggest policy making . but it have not powerful machinery of implementation of work due to role of indian constitution.. its solve only basic level social justice and empowerment . its have to seen in country practically s.c/s.t take 6o years to

reach in basic social justice . the indian constitution very great role the control of work implementation given the

judiciary with sufficient number lawyer (LL.B/LL.M) and medicine graduate /postgraduate degree(like

MBBS/MD)/profession to oppose castes person have sufficient number l.l.b/l.l.m and m.b.b.s/m.d /m.s skill to create a complex problem to promote of business , industory and tender which castes only have sufficient officers. which castes without sufficient number lawyer (LL.B/LL.M) and medicine graduate /postgraduate degree(like

MBBS/MD)/profession have not possible to solve complex problem create by oppose caste which have sufficient number l.lb/l.l.m and m.b.b.s/m.d/m.s degree.

There are 2 to 3 type of social justice/empowerment 1. basic level 2.standard level 3.third level /higher level to promote large scale business ,industry . but only have to possible 1st level basic socialjustice by sufficient number bureaucracy in a castes itshave to understand by country india constitution and practicaly have to seen s.c/s.t take 65 yeras to rech basics level social justice not a problem of skills of peoploe but skills of problem of degree.

but which weaker section castes join sufficient number lawyer and m.b.b.s /m.d /m.s de- gree. solve standard level to higher level social justice/empower

-ment to promote of work in business /industry very easily in 4 to 5 years

4.gangster composition in india /which hindu religion individual castes have join sufficient number number lawyer (LL.B/LL.M) and medicine graduate /postgraduate degree(like MBBS/MD)/profession degree and safety of concerned problem

india which hindu religion castes castes have join sufficient number of number lawyer (LL.B/LL.M) and medicine graduate /postgraduate degree(like MBBS/MD)/profession .which castes envolve /composition gangster in india .with- out sufficient no. of lawyer and m.b.b.s/m.d/m.s degree. /degree profession have not possible to envolve/ composition of gangster in india. for the matter of attention/sense which hindu

religion castes have to face the problem of gangster in india and have not justification by court pending of castes in long time in court/with- out evidence have not favoure (justification).of victim. some time have not possible to reach the
court/ policies, due to create by gangster a complex problem.
.for the fight of india hindu religion individual castes/ backward individ- ual

castes face of above problem concentrate of the degree/profession of sufficient number number of lawyer (LL.B/LL.M) and medicine graduate /postgraduate degree(like MBBS/MD)/profession

.

THE END

MY OTHER BOOK HAVE PUBLISHED ON ONLINE SELF BOOK PUBLISHING COMPANY - CREATE SPACE AN AMAZON COMPANY,WEBSITEURL- https://www.createspace.com, COUNTRY-UNITED STATE OF AMERICA, ADDRESS- Seattle, WASINGTON, United States of America. ALSO ONLINE SHOPING AVAILABLE ON- www.amazon.in (COUNTRY-INDIA), www.amazon.com AND e-book kindle version on www.amazon.com and www.amazon.in

BOOK NAME- 1. Global Conflict: Capitalism, Communism and Wisdom of Mind of Peoples and Its Option Paperback(ISBN-13: 978-1503096745 AND ISBN-13: 978-1503084353

- **ASIN: B00P9SMWU4**

2. Osho Rajneesh a Review: Osho Wisdom Fraud Philosopher /Yogi Have to Produce Failure People Paperback
- ISBN-13: 978-1505297089
3. Some Interesting Topic on Human Right Worldwide and

Country: Country Europe / U.S.A individual Peoples Option of Standard Level Business
* ISBN-13: 978-1505336696

MY OTHER EDITION OF THE BOOK-- country India Hindu religion individual castes /s.c/s.t / o.b.c weaker sections immediate - poverty solution, increase huge business , industry ,tender ,social empowerment ,human right very-very big role join individual castes sufficient number lawyer (LL.B/LL.M) and medicine graduate /postgraduate degree(MBBS/MD)/profession have published on online self book publishing company- www.pothi.com ,country-INDIA(Address-BANGLORE),also online shopping available on that website URL.

THANKS FOR READER.

NEXT   EDITION   COMING   SOON